CAST DICE

CAST DICE

ALARI ALARE CELINE

CAST DICE

iUniverse books may be ordered through booksellers or by contacting:

iUniverse
1663 Liberty Drive
Bloomington, IN 47403
www.iuniverse.com
1-800-Authors (1-800-288-4677)

ISBN: 978-1-4917-8578-2 (sc)
ISBN: 978-1-4917-8577-5 (e)

Library of Congress Control Number: 2016903045

Print information available on the last page.

iUniverse rev. date: 08/29/2016

Contents

Burning Vow

The sacrosanct oath,
Burning vow.
Release the entire universe.
Puissant as the past terrific tsunami.
Cozily arduous, and on also on.
It is a hitch, knot.
Have the house,
Firm and a home.
The plot of a graveyard.
E'en cemeteries overcrowded by crisis.
Existence brought the coffin,
Brought trees and carpenters.
Immediately you came; it was made.
Cast on, the patent genial discourse
On the throttled be felling vow. And
All about the plot!
Not even the knowledge on their squelch!
I will demonstrate to you how to regard
The principles—or if not entirely.
To the by-standing downtown peddlers.
They who prove nonpareil. Call upon
The squadrons and all of their associates,
All the unsuccessful and the misled cohorts,
Those who belonged to the downtown bordellos, who
Floundered dignity in drinking jamborees.
Be set, cast.
Cast, in all the possible loopholes. And through
The glacial text that maimed the paratroopers.

Wait! All this will come and be.
Get healed from moral deficiency.

The sacrosanct oath,
Burning vow.
The adulterous brain. Sobriety
Ties the knot tightly.
I correct you slightly.
Signatories of the burning vow,
You put on a crest and a helm
Engaged in a joust. So
The lance ready on the launched attack.
Vowed to betray the worst,
Marveled on tactical supremacy,
Avowal of the dreary headway
Have won the ruffian badge.
Like who didn't understand the contents
Contained in the red accord.
To those who understood. Accolade,
The trophy of fidelity.
Patience, in its state of recognition.
Who cares about dilapidated boys and girls?
Malnourished, unlettered progenies?
This will still be the talk of tomorrow.
I die tomorrow.
The rigor of the drawn-out vow,
Means of the morning rise,
Promotion of the concept of existences,
Not for your good. Also I
To encounter the tranquil distant happiness. Safety!
Burning vow.

Tears of Anger

These series of the unending episodes.
Beyond the pale and the jaded ghost of continuity on me.
Yelling to curse the cruelty and the non-declining desires.
I know; I could be acting as the ancient risen mummy.
I am crying to the height of my diminishing will.
You have just derided my consciousness; my soul is homeless.
Stealing all my clothes and exposing the most protected treasure.
They laughed continuously and shamelessly, pointing right at my pride.
Why couldn't you even house their eyes, ballooned hearts, or even their
    un-wanting will?
Thought was in consideration, was only fit for the sty.
Only to scramble for the least with the farm animals.
I wonder the one who named and considered the good of you.
That day I will address on your deflated, egotistical endeavors.
I sternly cast aspersions on you, in making them look down on me.
Even the very intimate rejected the prize of sweetness,
Thinking fit enough to rob their glued attention for a while.
I stand to disown all men who surround me.
I am crying to the height of my diminishing will.
Am slowly throwing up, reserve the dozy nightly pill
Or any solution of any sort to push it down my failing gullet.
You acknowledge the merits of my pallid face.
I now down the every kind of tool.

I won't engage in any commotion of any nature whatsoever.
Rush hastily and come to my rescue.
You've just lashed my soul and my spirit, bleeding profusely.
Kindly hold my hands—I can no longer see—
Before I crack my nails on the tiny pebbles.
Before I dress, lock me inside a room for no more exposition.
Expel me from the unending spirits of generations
Of those who never consecrated their fate.
Cast this heavy laden to those who crippled my broadened shoulders.
If only the will and the desire are not in immeasurable rejection.
Shelter and coach me on how to behave well.
Where else can I run to?
For I know am an outcast, banished from all riches of the monarch.
I just want to hold their cracked lips, not to even smoke out a word.
I know that my fate is doomed.
I am crying to the height of my diminishing will.

Poor Soul

Malignant malefactor,
The benefactor
Of oceans and tides,
The golden and silver empire.
Gods of the beneath.
Towering and magnificence,
Laborious and idleness,
A hall in darkness.
Fame of sadness.
Not accorded
Fool's paradise.
The night owl.
Poor soul.
Tongue, a man's sword
Like a stone bridge.
Only, be assured of safety.
In peril of owns,
Guard from the wishful.
Once in,
Already in pact
As Scylla and Charybdis.
Pacification,
That dirty thing.
Captive Ata Amata.
Panicked, the outskirts
For no ransom.
Crusty patriarch.
Precious gone limbs and privacy.

No more Ata Amata.
Culled his livestock
For more, he thought.
I will say,
"You are so timely,"
Mauled by riches' satire.
Ruined the compassion.
Found on delusion.
Creator created
That weak track.
Fluid of dejection,
The endangered vessel.

Prudence

Daughter of Ndagla,
He is here for you.
To fly you home with him,
You cast the antique, poisoned arrow,
Not dreading the contentious merchant,
Letting out his hidden secrets.
Great huntsman of his day
Rode home on high.
Not even Prudence's
Amulet can disguise the opaque.
It's all on you.
Princess of Omia Diere,
Garments dried on the line,
Put on, to shelter.
The comb—search in the thatch.
Disfigures the prudence.
This might soon jolt my heir.
Take us to that privileged place
That restored your birthright.
Ne'er blame me, Ndagla, daughter of Prudence.
Aquamarine—all I had, Princess.
All jewels not for the ordinary settlers.
The lake is angry,
Consequential disobedience to sailors.
Otia not,
Not ruin your home.
"Be good. Leave me."
Hooting caused by hibernation.

Cast in the finger.
Silence the existence of down forces.
Whirls and whistles show that existence.
Dumped during stampede.
No knoll that can ever shelter the dead.
Open, strange is plagued.
Strange to Otia.
Prudence, you not knowing
The strength of prudence.
It which led the dog to the corpse,
Corpse decaying beside the ditch,
Ditch where travelers hid their treasures,
Treasures that caused the princess,
Prudence, princess of Omia Diere.

Feedback

Songs that wailed the heart. Like
The moon that shone at the far east of the continent,
Casting away horrifying fear of death.
Enraptured, seraphs close to the dream gate,
Arousing the feel of a well-heeled daybreak,
Unruffled as the flow of the alluring cascades.
To my dearest Solenko,
The rain is torrential.
Supposed this laced the infinite pleasure.
I gave you all, assumed I ought to have all.
For those unseen barbicans of the majesty,
Forgetting was only for the dreamland.
Tears rolling as the Malengo village's tributary.
I will still write my feedback
To rekindle the lost moments
That wrapped me in that silk garment,
Just torn before the late-evening dinner.
Geared noisome sights.
The stream of invective
Piercing, the now inflamed heart.
My spirit will soon flee from this land
And away from Granny's paddocks.
And the protracted endurance?
So damp and quaking.
The fest and styling.
That sweet and sweat.
Swelling the caged elation.
I will still write my feedback

To heal the persistent ulcer.
So contagious and diminished, all races.
Cast off the unfastened, rusty braces.
Take away the titanium handcuffs.
Not deserve,
Might go septic,
The antiseptic.
Pick up the tweezers.
Rise up
As smoke in a raging blaze.
Disengage the aging dissimilarities of kindred,
Caused by banging the unattended exit.
If not so,
I will still write my feedback.

If Only I Could

If only I could be allowed to talk,
I could talk about this charming place,
To express the bliss in my smokeless voice,
To show the atmosphere of this master sky,
To share the amazement of the starry night.

If only I could take to the air,
I could smell the priceless, adamant pain,
To live not to dispense disparity,
To keep the rhythm, not to flap unvaryingly,
To pull down continuous, discordant rendition.

If only I could walk alone,
I could cast my shadow aside,
To swim loose and surf progressively,
To traverse and strengthen marine ties,
To lie inside the tomb, awaiting departure.

If only I could express unevenness,
I could open the lumpy and bumpy chests afore,
To show what the world has hid inside,
To crack and depict incalculable agony,
To recognize the sacrifice of the discrete misogynist.

If only I could be consented to sing,
I could have put to task the harmonica and the mouth organ,
To heckle the souls of sinners locked in purgatory,
To sing the harmonious hymns of the centuries,

To cast out the spell of intolerance.

If only I could speak of indifferences,
I could have spoken about the day after the next day,
To bring out the cryptic, endless, melodious speech,
To cuddle them off the famous speech disorders,
To stand at the podium and boast beastly at the dome.

If only I could be asked to make a prayer,
I could benevolently invoke the oracles at the creek,
To reestablish the mislaid spirits of exuberance,
To reawaken the fresh and trendy standards of this date,
To soon back up the multicultural realm.

If only I could be,
I could have triumphed in everlasting victory,
To stroke and bathe loosely before the honorary,
To bask in the technocratic assembly of pity,
To be—if only I could.

And the Touch Went Out

Howl not.
Tears reserved, all-powered.
Bawl not.
Peace, the Almighty.
Happy be blessed,
Poor in spirit.
Heaven,
Thy kingdom come.
Mourners of unlikeness,
Behold the kindness,
Rapport of the only occasion.
To be filled as they flow.
Blessings they flow,
Pleasure of the inculpatory heart.
Pure in, be heart.
Meet him, the one after hefty hassle,
For the lengthy interview before we part home.
Love you, as I, the must-touchers.
Affirm, building the word.
Taste of that good salt.
Hit down the great fault.
It not again,
Not for the soils of the vineyard
Thrown in Malacca amidst canes.
Listen, my ears, do you?
On completion of the tower.
Tiny crystals on the shore
At the far end of the flat.

The city hill that was ne'er hidden,
Where tatty helpers were massively battered.
It does; the light is.
Not e'en the accomplished masqueraders.
Plain pact! Be one you could.
Fortress invisible in the parklands.
Indefatigable light, salient on high hills.
Only he lives higher in the towers.

Poetical Bonanza

And the rise of the moony light,
And the sparkle of the stars at night-crack.
Let me write you a poem within a poem,
And it be a story within a story.
And all swallowed at the wink of sundown
The sudden grief on its bleak sighs.

And when the sun sets,
Still rest on officious, guileless prairie,
With the nighttime mist signed up.
Arise, still and stunned.
Applaud.
And the garden-fresh, magical gala?

Early morning waves and tides
Strangled in the depth of the oceanic waters.
Sabbatical astronomers in fully colored orchestra pants.
And the poetical bonanza?
All the historical baffles and hullaballoos.
I say they are elites.

Then if so,
The uncalculated flow and the stringed, clamored knish,
And the greatest wish?
Will they single out and undo?
But the excommunicated college of the saints-to-be bishops?
And the bonanza?

Molten Pot

Compulsive as language, a tool,
A mirror of our real picture.
These words,
Labeled that we thought they could be.
I'm already gone. Only
Collect me,
In order.
In need of knowledge acquisition,
Pulverize the immediate admiral.
Punctilious of the instant aftermaths,
The way of that life, long lived.
Occidentals reminiscing the shattered shuffleboard,
Remains best of all.
Its
Virtual dictatorial measures,
Terrifying miscarriage of justice.
You must, mustn't.
Now, the flow of politeness.
I'm already gone. Only
Smitten by the beauty.
Conceal me from the regicide
In the shroud of Turin.
To be hid from the Old Bailey.
Splendid chance before the disastrous tornado.
Hooey it is,

In the smokeless zone at the ozone,
From another kind of pollution.
Sieve,
For the fine.
Explicable.
Tacit.
Our own explicit.
Vision,
Morals inclusive.
Still holds as the responsible one,
On and on as the marine of riches,
For succession not of imitation.
I'm already gone. Only
Stranded before the rerun
On seeing the ogre on board.
Not the vagabond, you disoriented recruit.
If not for,
I speak,
Ban all the explosives.
Pick me up.
Could be uncanny, and of all ages
A treasure.
Molten pot.

Discontent

Democracy on horns of dilemma.
Yes, money-men.
Why not you?
Just a framework
Like active demos on move,
Stilling the interior décor, vending paucity.
The imaginary, traumatized monumental.
Today you have to talk about this place,
The slow pace of revolution,
And the unbecoming fetish hideouts.
The biscuit makers are also out,
Out to gag before entangled.
Big, sucking bottles, the big babies.
They've cast dice; back frazzled in completion.
And the dice watchers' beavering onslaught.
Pushing bottle tops on the draughtboard.
Providers of the pillars to the tower of strength
Grant the long awaited tutelage.
The decades-old lease.
Out of order, to speak. So
Swallow the sputum to clear for audibility.
Hump is too small for recognition.
May you protect the oasis
As the yellowed milk for the infants?
Kids, act before the after-play exhaustion.
Talk of questers in inadequacies.
A trespassing voice of that thing,
Logics limping, already crippled.

Ideologies in the buff, this heavy exposition.
Injudicious sentiment of pity; relish not
Flopping mayhem,
Arousing criticism.
The fatty and lean,
The hide and skin.
The date is yours to balance
In the guise of harmony.
Before the great confusion in the convoy of trails,
Purchasing the right for a few pence.
This is where cash is baked.
Now, cussword spoils the broth.
Not entice or cajole as small ones.
Reserve the peek-a-boos for the next sessions.
It will be a long-term endless nightmare.
All will be at that endpoint.
Mystery might only infuse the hope.

Nightfall Mardi Gras

Part 1

And when the sable hazes fall,
It rains—hails too, fall.
And the tightened waders get drizzly,
Away down the descending terrain.
We have the hollow waders print.

Jamming, the youth-looking faces
On the cleared, moist transom.
Twilight roses fall, face the gravel,
Waning grandeur in the hamlet.
And after the blizzard?

Lest you chuckled and slammed,
Waving unsolicited union banner,
Bursting out the favela.
Sneaking in supreme transgression
To dole out indemnity.

For the sudden sporadic encounter.
Now, stumping the war waders,
Shuddering in the wrecked perplexities,
Blatantly in the extraordinary mantra.
And the nightfall Mardi Gras?

When all recedes,
Takes off the crimson trilby,
When all dawn aids withdrawn,
Soon they had to leave,
To be back in the succeeding commiseration.

Part 2

When the dawn aids reinstate,
See, the waders are mud-spattered
In their weather-beaten sou'westers.
When the trilbies lower down
Scars of scalds on their noodles.

I think they'll slam and reopen,
Surge to the very placating place,
Masking the unsettled conundrum.
Will they look back and consider?
We cannot tell.

Sleep on this,
A nightfall on the frosty portico.
And the potbellied commanders?
A glimpse through the colored bifocals
With hands circled the paunch.

And for the beer-bellied generals?
Rotating hands in coinages.
Existing in creeps of the untold,
In whirls of the foretold.
What will they do when time approaches?

And if the entries are permanently bolted?
Will they smash out the pivots?
Or unshackle the bagged fundamentals?
Or tumble over for comfort?
Think about this.

Part 3

Go ahead. Call on the grand wardens
To un-blemish the mud-spattered cask
And construct the firm dais,
Giving senses to the irregular genre
In the midst of the rundown crunch.

Spacing adjacent, the chilled porch,
Waving the mud-spattered rag,
Pushing the scores to the barbed edge.
Soon, the soother will open and slam,
Exposing the flouted child's way.

Amazingly,
All the misgivings and the bloopers!
Uncertainty of the strident melodies
Soon wobbles,
Out of the unpacked, assorted brandies.

All overwhelmed in ecstatic tolerance,
And almost immediately,
Milliners will crotchet a dozen trilbies
And salvage all the weather-beaten
From all electoral porters.

Scores go silent,
Moaned grisly on dusk fall,
On gashing escapade.
Will they really understand?
Upholding sympathetic cessations.

Foolish Scholar

An ambulance.
No siren.
Already aural,
It's the dead lecturer.
Than demise.
Button up;
Conceal the unkemptness.
You, autodidact,
As on a chess board,
No survival.
It for the king.
Make a fuss over not.
Have learnt,
As an average pawn.
You knew,
Knew first.
Every market
Constitutes the two fools
Haggling for too much.
Too little is enough.
Raced for success,
That oblivious track.
Noxious one,
Lead again.
Gates to jail.
"I will grant the bail."
Inadequate sop to conscience.
Defiled the principle.

Autocrat
Broke her virginity.
They knew
A fool's errand.
Poacher!
Leave the lion.
Now,
Can't stop it.
Safeguard the prey.
Nothing as powerful as wrath
Of them.
They saw.
You oppressed.

Poem in April

Poem of the fourth
Verve in the alumni's congress.
Well done after the exertion.
You, the penniless agent. Stern.
Leisure's be laid in those deep soils,
Dissolved by acidity.

Knocked house to house,
Stripped garrulous cynics,
Showed snaggle-teethed wailers.
Not match the decency.
Slavishly redeemed from captivity.
Brought back activity.

Exposition of weakness,
Effects of concupiscence.
They who bargained for bed,
Bed that belonged to housemates,
Failed to house a member,
Ashamed the fire brigade.

Poem that embraced reconciliation
In April,
Month of harvest,
The exculpation of detainees
To massage excruciation through the bumper.
After long term under castigation.

Poem of illuminati,
Pea brained, "the high and mighty."
Cassoulet composed the belly,
Enlightens, the rhythm of edibility.
Poem of the deceitful brainstormed,
Heard on completion of summit.

Crestfallen pauperism,
Objurgation of dispirited natives,
Downgrading the norms,
Purely nostalgic concussive.
Emaciation after obliteration,
Debunk the nefarious will.

For the unborn in April,
Sanctified cost of the poem.
Keep it till the poem,
The crucial arithmetic solved.
Not you be fooled on the first day.
No one can elucidate being.

The determined hunter,
Not be afraid of thorns,
Relieve from the grip,
Heavily and pounding,
Recipient of the condolence.
Errand of mercy.

Of our times,
Sympathy in April.
Crème de la crème,
Secret and mysterious,
Not of talisman,
Poem in April.

Another Batterer Like You

The wrecked batterer, you are out-figured.
You slyly trawled in self-pity.
I mean, look at all these academia misconceptions.
Drawing gullibly toward the corps
In the sizzling tux! You've dressed the evil.
Not you deserve the cocktail, punch, or merely a parade of smoothies.
And the most wanting aroma of chicken breasts and bacon?
Not even a cleaner, least in the diplomatic escort.
You disgust, mysterious, wild cat. How about
Another batterer like you?

Mangled the feminine, fragile, black chin.
Disabled the unarmed hands that also fed you.
Boarded down and pulled to bits the right femur.
You liveth among the dead and the deadliest.
I ask,
Where do you belong?
Mauled the whole part of your world and gluttonously swallowed the
    freedom in it,
Only to burn in nonconsumable fire
To the un-suggested degree. Imagine it could be
Another batterer like you.

Will set and regulate the unbearable skeptic source
To the house-warming heat in the potential spell.
You've seen her through the mega transition,
Shut down completely the will to carry on.
Do you think it's on time to withdraw the boisterous cat?

So indecisive though. But
I must say, it's long overdue.
You will now feed on cockroaches for dinner. And
House the obstinate lice and those reeking jiggers. Waiting for
Another batterer like you.

Orphan's Song

Us and us alone.
New form and perspective.
Still young and witty.
Pa, you are thirteen.
You are still young.
We grow old.
Younger than them, you borne,
Tears down to fill the void bowl.
Orphan's song.
Quarantine for the thirteen years
Might last forever.
Naive also, Ma.
Seven only.
Please, only a glass,
Be it of water,
Juice for appreciation,
I will bless you.
I am in tatters,
Bout to exhaust,
Spirits of hard work.
They pierced,
Pierced the painful parts,
Only with the eyes,
Past the ill-omened apparels.
They displayed travail.
Tears down all over the face.
Mucus down the nostrils.
Say hello to know your existence.

What if I meet you?
Not an excellent resolution.
For if I,
Who will use my hoe?
An extra hoe?
Additional pain and agony.
Come, call me
For the hidden secrets.
I was not informed.
Said it half,
Half of the story.
Who will?
The two, you must be guilty.
Who will sow the seeds?
Holes too deep.
Hoe too big.
For bigger hands it belonged.
Only two
In need of eight
To do it ourselves.
Ran away from us,
Left the wild to feast.
You left the hoe since,
Ne'er had it rained.
Disappeared are also rain clouds.
Bring them down.
When felt upon by all,
Recollecting the random hitting of the clubs,
Sang stroking in discomfort,
Sang in rows placing to rest,
Some swaying and dancing,
Some highest to top of their voices.

Beauty of the dirges
Only to welcome the "visitors."
Wake up. We adore
All from hand to mouth.
Battling for the leftovers or none.
No importance of the occasion,
As donkeys, pulling carts of affliction.
Not for us it couldn't.
Forever it will be a song,
Orphan's song.

A Comeback

The antiseptic
Might go septic.
Up with the tweezers
To cleanse the ulcer.
I received
Feedback.
A comeback.
Have felt the pinch,
The outspoken tune,
Like a dream,
Once upon a dream.
Full of fortunes, shrouded by kniphofia.
Had the thick ma's bouillon.
Only for protection and safeguarding.
Heard it all—all.
And keeping it real?
Imagine the taste of the humbled delicacies
Before the modish cavalcade.
Discovered being ulcerative,
I denied the real.
Now, denied the sleep.
Stirring the saturated cold
Caused pain in heart,
Much labor for the pain.
Empty, endless laughter
Sandwiched between.
Inside is killing.
Slowly it can put off.

Down on knees,
Accept the beggar,
Shouts of a foolish emperor.
I promise to ne'er—
Ne'er the one I could e'er find.
Down on me from heaven.
I will cherish the thoughts.
Going up the stair,
Loosen the stare.
Caused ulceration.
Be under medication.
Allow me if only,
The heart desires the knock.
Knock for a comeback.
I will do it gently,
Rub the floor neatly.
Let me have you.
Listen to the enemy.
Before the hurricane,
I will channel the waters
Ahead of the heavy downpour.

Heroes' Corner

Long-term dreams of the hopefuls,
Dreams of our forefathers,
Of makers of great nations.
Revelation of the classic dream,
The lengthy knight's dream.
> "I have a dream that one day
> This nation will rise up and live
> Out to the true meaning of its creed."

The audacity that revealed the dream,
> "Yes we can."

Genesis of the thirsted freedom,
Forty-fourth,
The crucial, sudorific lineup.

Freedom to being free.
Though, it will tomorrow.
Lay hopes in one row,
Strangled by all the possibilities of purchase.
For twenty-seven, we are free.
Years when Nelson
Cast the sheathing from the halfwits,
Brought back the prize of excellence
For the desperate,
The champs who wept,
Wept that stained as blood.

Angel of mercy and
Saint of the gutter.

Fled all hopes to Calcutta.
Charity is free, love priceless.
Consent the engorged hearts
Not e'en too poor to love.
Shalom,
Joy, well lived.
On the tenet of that dream,
Weaved on the weighty ambitions,
Attached those in seclusion.

Wet blood spilled on the barren land,
Steady with the lifelong battle
Against users of anabolic steroids.
Arsenal prior to the prep of Armageddon.
To save those who live,
Who feel the sweetness and gratification
Of the ancient, alien alcopop.
This is for our children. Also
Grand and great-grand of this unfortunate race.
Can we give back the bassinets?
>"The challenge is to restore the home
>Of tadpoles and
>Give back to our children
>A world of beauty and wonder."
Stunt the churlish conference of classism.
By flattery, tales of the hummingbird. Doyenne
Won them through peace and power.
Later, you shall experience the goodness.
Mystery of the long-downcast environment.

"I greet you, my people."
Wisdom to prevail in our lives,
Already through with the exigence.
No longer have we had the empty room,
The ruined, the violated destitute.
I intend to inform,
Great men never extinct.
Still on this legacy burns
Like bush fire with no premonition,
Jovial king of intellects,
Appreciation of the earned exposure,
E-governance, E-learning, name all …
Applauded by the great senate of Rhodes.
Comrades,
"I might be back."
Back with heroes peeping at the corner,
Casting detrimental effects of the abandoned onlookers.
Long since this voice came up.
"I am free."
"I may be back."

(In memory of the late Alari Alare Kenneth.)

Discriminating Call

Deserted.
Am alone.
Leave me.
Fed up.
No more.
Why did it?
That little one.
Ain't a solecism.
You or he?
Negotiation before
Murky.
Not ecstasy.
Trammel sojourn.
Run but hide not.
Discriminating call.
Betrayed naivety.
Empty slate.
I be the guttersnipe.
No specific destination.
I comply,
I bore
The bastard.
Unable to hold
As a milksop.
Exorcize
In the arms of Morpheus.
Wake up.
Take up.

Fatigues of Augean stables.
Outrageous nomenclature.
Foe, the description.
Responsibility essence.
You deserve
Feasible atheist.
I'm poor.
Clean your face.
Cleanse this shame.
Discriminating call.

My Confidant

With the never-ending poetical messages of my confidant.
With the vexing lyrics of misery and the smart, strategized blathers.
Today give me the exclusive mouthwatering,
Not the usual breathtaking natters.
Are you under any sort of unidentified influence or what?
Today you will sing of the streaming wonders in Nyaribo,
With the glimmering sounds of the old Mabiko round tune,
Shredding down my drum into doubtful pieces.
On Tuesday will be all about the miscarriages in Kabiongi.
You will screw your face, and all this ends up in profound despondency.
The next day's wedding at Maili Mbili.
Boogying jauntily to the pricking tune of the xylophone.
You have briefed me of violence in the rogue Dwenda.
Today is on Thursday.
Only to stand aside, chanting songs of war,
Not even a sign for truce.
"Did you know of the sendoffs in Nyakiusa?"
Every Friday, Mr. Confidant.
Doom and gloom as we lower our departed heroes,
With the well-knitted rope just for this celebration.
Early morning Saturdays, the usual sweetness of the traditional brew in
    Torenko.
Hopping to the famous beats and wetting down pants as toddlers.
Unomi sacrifices on calm Sundays in midafternoon.
Appease the demigods for all the occurrences in Salengo state.

You know my friends and their friends.
I am covertly looking for my confidant's confidant,
To learn the sorrows, the wholesome—perhaps your wedding day.
Kindly just tell me,
Who will inform me of your departure?
I would wish to eulogize and cover up for the pocket-sized secrets
And to design the unalloyed epitaph,
To cover in crude, unfathomable, poetical briefs.
You are in deep grave danger.
Expose me to your friendship; I want this in your clemency
If I truly am your confidant.

Toss the Coin

Countable slaps roll down,
The long percussion awaited.
Extreme furnish to the janitorial
Just before the midday arrivals.
What you ought is what,
For I be what I ought to,
Not a nit to be squeezed.
Clean out the disgusting brown dust
For the flawless audition.
No niggling.
Toss the coin.
Royalists smeared their faces with dessert,
Dirtying the white-collar garments.
All not well. And
Again we must ring the bell.
Ringing with superb difference.
The formal official diary is
Sign in, sign out. Open
The diary of debtors
For you and for me.
Victims on grand collision
Unable to put the emptiness,
Void under the unusual circumstances.
Look at the hemispheres
As the sharp, pointed spears.
Concrete, forbidden solutions.
For the chin-waggers of neurological complications.
We'll all die in the coming days.

Not trace the shadows.
Salvation is laid in rows.
Strangulated on principles and situation.
Out of the cursed bush,
Fished out in an instant ambush.
Hard to crack.
It's inside.
Radical transition shows its essence.
Clear this fast, ever-growing green bush.
We are both the bargaining casualties;
One most suffers the pain, we must
Toss the coin.

Licking Porridge

Seal the bowl.
Clean the deal.
Why?
Spares not.
Apparent hole of oppression.
Crevasse of segregation.
Tunnel of phobia.
Heart of consciousness.
Burning hearth.
Hot as furnace.
Lethal is
Downtrodden bowl.
Enlarge the alleyway.
Fallacies to brim.
Ostentatious.
Form of racism.
Downhearted taste.
Deserted, which isn't,
Discriminating tone of monotony.
Dahomeans,
Smart and adaptive.
Not the happy-go-lucky,
The improvident.
New bowl purchase.
Stop the porridge licking.
It newly accommodates.
Outcome be shame.
Impact be anguish.

Bowl of pleasure,
Enrich the porridge.
Establish the new urn
To lunch alfresco.
Alleviate disgust
Exorbitant to maintain.
Make a trial,
Wipe the salty tears,
Curse the fears.
Need affection,
Prevention,
Licking porridge.

Son of Mikayi

First of the first
Son of a woman.
The woman who disposed the gods,
god to the woman.
With his touch,
Held the swords of lightning,
Slaughtered the huge, red cock
Whose crow frightened Sakewa.
Only with the stare,
Rivers stood still.
Still one's meandered.
Drunkards pissed like children.
The deaf ran of sensation.
Dogs immediately to their kennels.
His dance paved way,
The vigorous twists.
All the mist cleared went so clear.
Skin shredded into slices. Down
Traditional Migosi's drum.
Swiftly, they dashed out of the harem.
His smile,
Harmony in the whole of Sakewa.
Handsome of Mikayi,
A blink spoke for the feelings.
Women shrieked like mad ones.
Pigeons cooed for strong relations.
Smothered the strong men,

This man silenced the flowing rivers. That
Scared a woman,
Who trained the great son,
Son of Mikayi.

Illicit Brew

Bloody vicinity,
Illicit bred.
Demons of tussle
Maintains only disarray.
Tree surgeon,
Diagnose it—
The tree of knowledge.
Big spoons be big,
Not small spades
Misunderstood.
Scrawny.
Objection.
Perplexingly detailed.
Detainee of no appropriate name,
Locked, in a lockup
That held illicit sinners.
You can't be proud and call them your own.
Only of this unfortunate setup,
They call it their own.
Eroded the way that
Was preserved for tomorrow.
Life, as in flammable tubes
Like addition of firewood,
The illicit liquor.
Moral bankruptcy,
The brew is bitter.
Pisses on cogitation,
A clear sign of obscurity.

Not realization,
Subsequent mayhem.
Wipe,
Specs of blindness.
Pour,
Spirits of the uncouth.
Dismantle,
The pot of injustice.
Extinguish,
The disastrous endless inferno. Shun
The deep-rooted, most obvious, and obvious.
The native's outcast illicit brew.

Peculiar Treasure

Arrows in a quiver.
Killed the flesh,
Not obtained the grape.
Blow is strong.
Heavy thud.
Dismantled pieces
To that invisible magnitude.
Disrespect for master.
Reason for tatter.
You're slaves not,
Not slaves,
Men of goodwill,
Peculiar treasure.
Not of them
Captured the ebullience.
Not have sunk
Tenants of yard.
You believed not
Now, rather say,
We surrender.
Away,
Thrown out of the vine.
Not enjoy wine.
"As you sow, so shall you reap."
Not maintain
All in pain.
Beauty now,
A catastrophe.

Marred by mishap.
Cannot slake the knocking hiccup.
Pulling a dray can never make you
The Kalahari's beast of the burden.
Have distinction.
Peculiar treasure.

This Day

This day I will shine
To supersede the societal misdemeanor,
Not to glare upon the setbacks
And intentionally hit the tectonic plates against another.
To render the bizarre seismic fright
To the undesirable level of obliteration,
Building the unprecedented faulting.
Yes, they will follow the steps
And dismiss the lone warriors with their cattle heads.
Let on and on the uninterrupted want.
Mmmmh … I want to dream in quietude
And achieve masquerading loudly on the onset.

This day I will shine,
Cherish those who took me 'round and not who in spirals
And join them in the return of the heads.
Am not a professional vet, rustler; this ain't an abattoir.
Only stride and swing in complete contentment
And to whisper deeply in intense,
                              "They are not complete men."
Spilling down the actual tone of my being
And listen when my ears can.
See when still unaided.
Move when the stick is not ready.
Laugh when my teeth can still block the ugly spaces
I will turn and tore.

This day I will shine
And explore the unreachable spaces.
To let go the ten and save the two,
I never want to be literary overwhelmed.
On this day of the nefarious storm,
The crew must have marked their way out
Before the forsaken boat capsizes.
Lighting up their club candles in secrecy before the escapade.
Of course, I know they won't be over the moon.
And the two?
As dangers loom?
This might on this day.

Make It, Be It

Don't abuse wine trappers.
It still persists.
Not throw dust in the eyes,
Antiquated.
Turn tables cannot.
What molded it'll
Each for a spree
Turn the new leaf over.
The goat, not the act.
Every door with its keys.
Not abhor the player;
The game, yes.
Vengeance wise not.
Remove the horsehair,
The bloated plutocrat.
Relinquish yapping.
Patience pays,
It to simmer
Lick not the ladle.
Not in order to skedaddle.
Remorseful repercussion.
So elapse minutes
Status irrespective of
Be it,
Molded by hands
Somewhat skullduggery.
One appears skuzzy.

All in limbo.
Built it firm,
The intellectual caliber.
One add one, never eleven.

If Not Now, Never

Take me to that foreign village,
To the defiance, infested descendants,
To see the glow and the sparks of Turiani woodlands.
The radiance from the evergreen source of contrition
Put the casing over my un-scarfed head.
And the wet cow dung under my feet,
From the gust and the striking lightning,
Engross me for the kitchenette prattles.
When will Wekusi trade?
Go out and unchain the gate.
They might knock till eternity,
And in the basket will have gone stale
And down at gale.
Draw the duchess out the harem.
Turiani! Perhaps later you will be in acceptance.
So many to ask,
But if by any chance you think they will allow her decompose in your soil?
And when they are wholly gone?
To only surround the yard in sugarcane plantations
For the humongous harvest at the end of the season.
Lead her through,
If not now, never even in death.

Dawn

Lit the innocence.
Splendid, dazzling suit.
Dignitary, the emcee,
Amazed by that touch.
Reflection of the environment.
Defaced the go-getters.
Scared that evil thing.
They who like fascinating
Take a pen.
She, the reticent kind
Put down yours.
Go on close.
I know
Everything is the wish.
Visible and also invisible.
Put down the huge eyelid
Also for the numerous minute.
Out with the modified abets.
Take it out.
Light the world.
Expresses its elegance.
You are hours old,
And you're not old?
Evidence to transparency
Up the spirit to reconcile.
Dawned on us.
Humbled those vigil musketeers
Who bombard, raided the primitive dominion.

They bellowed and echoed,
Pushed hard and cast the fierce tremor,
Crushed right into the dung-smeared house.
Dawned on us,
Silenced the empty rhetoric.
Earthly creatures ran for safety.
The sparkling, the blinding flare.
Sharks sunk into the great ocean.
Guards out after the grueling duty.
The usual enthusiastic cock's crow,
All at the crack of dawn.

Let Me Give Birth

I will bear the next generation of greatness.
I want to witness the sacrilegious, colic cries,
To wet and soil my polyester jeggings.
Let them breathe in me and out.
They will for themselves.

I want to cry again,
To wipe the tears out of pain
And to build the master chain.
I know they will soon ordain.
Let me give birth again.

I have to carry the fruitions of gratification
Of the veiled, distinguished mothers
Who looked up on a journey in desire,
Counting the entire fortunes in laughter,
Naming all their long-gone ancestors in fairness.

Who will ever remind me,
Let me run and play,
Let me hide, come and find me
In the long grass beside my sack-made bathroom
I was once a child.

Who will guard my home?
Roast my rich groundnuts,
Fetch water from the swollen Kamubelo River?
I ask, can I sneak in a helper?
My delicate back will soon go stiff.

Alas! When the day will be finally here,
They will burst out in utmost shock.
Who will groom me well?
And praise my mother.
I will be leaving. I have been called back.

Vanity

Oblivious of the common earth-shattering,
Insurmountable effects of its own.
Source of demise concealed.
And in the vanity case?
Of the pool of fortunes.
If only you could turn off the magical gravity,
Then all would be suffocated into space,
Also not of the common earth-shattering.
Tally up the aftereffects.
Enfranchise, this might be a kiss of death,
A threat of its kind.
I belong to it.
Observed the heliport in great wish,
Not robbed by social seclusion.
Malcontent mafioso of honeydew melon.
Shield the entire race against subjection.
Thinkers to earn protection,
Never be ruled by possession.
This swamp-bred vanity,
Not my permanent premises though.
Yes, all will come to pass.
Master of peace,

The avant-garde masterpiece.
Honor the deterrence trade.
Vanity of vanities, all vanity,
Vanity.

Resurrection

Indecent.
Sludge.
The soggy ground.
Caused imbalance.
May be facile
Ain't facets.
Resurrect.
Rise,
The crude one.
Mayn't in fad fashion,
No bourgeois values.
All in limelight,
Ululation still.
A hungry man. Angry
Molestation of sophisticated taste.
Tranquility through devotion.
Hereto,
Heal the wounds.
E'en falcons make hunters.
Introduction of the soup kitchen,
Not dillydally on nitty-gritty.
A tricky task, the forthright ombudsman.
Calm the rocking nuisance.
Most of all, founder of the domain,
Hold for the arrival; "big things are here."
A flop at this survival's most crucial fleck. For
Uncouth they are,
Ransacking of the royal, the precious throne,

Drooling and guzzling.
Puddings,
May it break?
Homeless, so the principled
Resurrect,
Abolish,
Law of the jungle.
Dump garbage not.
Free the eagle.
Decency
One to another.
Capitalism. Outstretch
Communal buries the burden.
Resurrection of the society
To preclude the possible discernible blast.
Here upon
In need,
Resurrection.

A Maniac

Gigantic.
Dancing as never.
Wrist, abdominal.
Magic powers,
Black boosters.
Dusk, dawn
On the peak of a hillock.
Rebellious haggard.
Squalid, regardless of squall.
Ekweni, he-devil
Like a steeplejack,
Mimic, renegade.
Squeaky as murmurs,
Adjacent to tombs.
Being foolhardy,
Playing the second fiddle.
A maniac.
Not even guts
Be a genuine one,
A complete fiasco.
Fierce and mischievous.
Short-termed dancer.
Faint heart never won.
Bravo, carry on.
E'en a bassoon,
That alluring pitch.
Sounds moronic.
For complete escalation,

Daily brews perfection.
Gain decorum,
Nearing ordination.
High expectations.
Dance.
Rock into frenzy
For stipulated limitations.
Major drawback,
Clinic aspect.
Wrestle phobia.
Tighten the bolts.
Make the dance.

My In-Laws

Those looks screeched beneath the windswept smiles.
As in sheer disgust in the greatest fright of the untold.
Let me nuzzle this child you raised for me.
Too little and in dire need of a concierge.
At this time, your duties are all nursed.
You frown in intense, just to scare the fancy.
Let me enjoy this, and finally,
Then, I shall write the most beautiful song
On that very night that you will open your hearts.
I will supplement in the mellowest tune
To the song that will tone your drive.
Let me lead the child to infinity.
Only allow the separable to come in between and declare,
"Now time has come."
Not a distant from the moment, yet
My beauty will have caused exhaustion at this time.
And I know you will soon surrender.
And at once when all conflicts are tightly caged,
Like the heavens, that will be the sweetest place.
Will treat those angels to the renowned ballet.
They will dance and dance finally,
To crown the next ballerina.
It shall be only
If you consent me fulfill my hallowed assignment.

Lend Them Your Ears

Abhorrence. Lend them your ears.
Cogitating to slain in abattoirs
For raising brows on tossed coins. We,
The prolific prize recipients, planchet makers,
Concealed under the gooey,
Condemned by the flashy.
The masked sympathizers.
Appearance be mange,
Armed with the sticky
Requisition of coins. Financier,
They miss pip-pin,
Abandoned trash stored in cans.
The luxurious à la carte.
They need to.
So how?
Like a shadow meadow,
The pint-sized who pipe dream
Observed in grotesque on arrival.
Ain't of abdication. Set the throne free.
Foul, not forged to hereditary.
We, amiable composers of life,
No one amenable
As fools opposed to interlocutory,
Not distinction of the real one.
Comprehension of the grotty being.
Drooling for the left.
Not the elands.
We elites,

Not in need of alms
To be heard.
Your nom de plume be registered
To grasp the abyssal, denied exposure.
Why not you expose it?
To feel the goodness,
Lend them. Sensitive as
The subsequent peril, adroit alarm
Disperses all and all, shreds up the proud heart
And every bit up in a gale.
Have to be quenched,
Long-term thirst of the diehards.
No ephemeral salads to confine the hysterical rumor,
To refresh the corner of indispensability.
A pinch of comprehension,
The pinch not be licked.
Effigy fancies on their noodles.
Egg them do something,
For we refuse to die.
This, a non sequitur.
Lend them your ears.

Kit-Mikayi

With the prying, strange tales of the massive rock,
Made her creased, silky face even more senile,
Battling this age in utmost quietude and reservations.
Let me know, I beseech.
Instill me with the dreadful tales of your time.

They thronged, as brought by rollers from the great lake,
Deftly as the bereaved, yet of disputes
Of pilferages, of the usual mind distortion.
Held tight like breakers on the coastline
Mending the frail, unmusical boom.

This's what I supposed on seeing Kit-Mikayi.
Besides Grandma's house on the hilltop,
Not even the minute sleet could hide on the top,
Not even ascribed by the mind-boggling stargazers.
I know it stained anticipations.

Oh yes, I overheard the unmusical boom.
They fell on their knees to be unfettered.
As the breakers on the coastline, they held.
Even if it could be for the plucking of the most painful hangnails,
Only the whistling birds came and even camped.

Even pushed in the immortal dene.
Tantalize! The greatest liars of our times.
Even moved in a stormy deluge.
Hark! The people will stunt and taciturn.
The legionnaires will still drum till the next daybreak.

Soldiers poised as members of the old school.
They not the church-, temple-, or even mosque-goers.
Not nonbelievers yet the irredeemable believers.
No concrete comment that broke the chain.
No positivity, contemplated not to leave even tomorrow.

All is up indeed. It's up; give up.
Have to be flexible and have to be
The famous figure of the western part and its parties.
One day you will heed this voice; this shall come.
I shall partly seize the earth, strategic points.

Phenomenon Philomena

Whip not
Baby girl. And also
Weep not baby.
Whistles impact not
The heretical buttocks.
You blew it. Now
Slogan of the ladder.
That whip begets weep.
Slow,
A compassion.
Pretty-pretty
Sophism intrusions.
Bring it, gigolo.
It's a yippee,
Yum, yummy ladder,
Tum, tummy tender.
Not a clerihew.
Just as frigid as ice cold.
The expression is down in the dumps.
Think about
Struggling out of a red-hot pan. Subsequently,
Diving at the core of an incinerator.
You are now proudly bestowed
Pageantry, the crown of tears.
Boys always and always they will be.
Civilly, gather the sores of humiliation.
Apartments are so untidy.
For three pence,

New brooms sweep.
You robbed Peter, paid Paul.
Waste not and want not,
The beauteous phenomenon.
Make dry feed at daylight
When the sun is austerely overhead,
And ahead of the snowy winter,
Still waters run wildly underneath.
Superior, above all the Amazon rangers.
Do well, phenomenon Philomena.

Dance of Death

A macabre.
Bovine scourge.
Not.
Lurid, not a lute.
Lyrically composed.
Showing no pair of heels.
Reflect *p*s and *q*s
Play fast not and loose.
One's dander raises.
Throw up never the sponge.
Nip in the bud suppose?
Lead in the garden some.
Throw on; cold water
Erase won't grotty noddle.
Blaze the trail.
Subsequently, chew the fat.
Strike the hot iron.
Not hold one's tongue.
Just knock on the head,
Accentuation responsibility e'er yours.
Cause of desire,
Consequences being dire.
Be entwined in a quagmire.
Things be haywire.
We are the higher.
Stop the alarming fire.

Dream

What that dream
Never dreamt.
This day,
Never this to ever appear.
Darkness falling down in an instant.
This is between you and me.
The first dream,
Who had it first?
Dream about me tomorrow,
After the long, tiresome race.
Sometimes before I am down.
Maybe you'll cover me,
My weakness in the glamorous flowers,
Returning dust to the same dust.
Wait for my dreams,
The phobic, legendary dreams.
Inside the squalid grandma's hut
That was smeared before sunrise.
Pass through the undone thatch
To reveal so real, real.
Release with gallows humor.
I'll walk with your hearts,
Wade in those shallow waters,
To the eastern-most part of the continent,
Only to warn and care for you.
Aren't you lucky?
Put the dream safe.
Learn, let it guide.

To sort the somber, tone out the voices,
Not to scare and misplace. Not
Cause galumph in the simple, sweet stay.
I first dreamt.
That dream.

Shade No Tears

Not a martyr by oneself.
Cynics or sycophants?
Who killed them?
Sacrificial of wish,
Thrashed in an open arena.
Is it of proven theories?
Clarified hypothesis?
As the Sapir-Whorf?
Thousands martyrs.
Crops confusion.
Who is he?
He be haughty?
The isolated ones?
In agonies of fellow men,
Living in your respect.
If there's resurrection,
Demise by circumstances.
Staccato of bullets
Breaking the silence.
Spit saliva on
Strong conviction,
Slave of freedom.
Slaved by
More pathetic,
Principled as Galileo.
Vivid pass of martyrdom.
Believing in
Demise of conviction.

Not battered by it,
Slaved by
Resurrection, they'll
Not killed.
If, who killed them?
Innocent blood.
Shade no tears.

Grotty Sperms

The glints of those hostile mourners,
Faded luminescence of the moon.
Executioner who weaved noose,
Triggered the strong nasal sensation.
Marred the man-eater who
Drove carelessly out of the hideout.
Hot for this usual lunch eaters,
Perturbed the whole that opposed the midnight agenda.
Branded the spectrum is purple, pink, peach.
Poinsettia, for the flora and fauna.
Long revealed by the latter fundamentalists.
On that very distant end of the quay.
All the conceit lapsed into intermittence.
Pestilential reoccurring syndrome.
Melodramatic arena with perverseness.
This sperms bought darkness and blindness.
Castles that almost touched the sky,
Pied–à–terre to the local gentry.
Cast away medieval, illuminated manuscripts
Out of marauding escapees.
I wish, the beggar.
Horses, the affluent.
Eviscerated on the pretext of flatulence.
Perjury was before the jury.
Martyrs of the greatest "blessings."
You spoke the same, the same that
Intoxicated the ordained amateurs.
Building up lunatic asylum on destined suburbs.

Prophets at two.
After midnight, cast to dogs bodies.
On the pulpit with the highness,
On the periphery of social dogma.
The dummies that designated the auspicious occasion.
Bran that was only left for the next morning.
This pen to rhapsodize the mission.
Neither the supreme antagonist that blocked with barricades
Nor the extremist who chanted slogans under coercion,
Only a peasant who peeped for the rodeo tourney.
Fix the denture.
Cast away the lent smile.
Not speak of firm revolution.
If not cast the hatred that dwelt.
Not the belief e'en when the sun set.
Strength with passion pushed hard and fell the walls.
Resolution after the ordinary tea party.
Experience the moving force of change.

Rejected Coin

The heart of peace that open the heavens
In a glade of the befogged curse.
A sacrilege let to suffer and the rejection?
The strength of that e'er-recursive foundation.
Cornerstone for the glamorous summer fiesta.
Take me,
My destination.
Take me,
Where I belong.
I need to.
Jurisdiction of the dismayed builder.
The plan be laid well for the chalet.
The hag, the hag-ridden.
Are these the clatters of reticence?
This might, the lingering hostility.
Dismissed, awful, the scorned desperado.
Later, award the ruined boy.
May well be like waft that pommel the universe.
Be out of naive realism, of those stars surrounding at moonlight.

Spit it out, the feral bard,
For the incensed in ire discolored their regalia.
Perverted conviction right to enkindled destination.
Unusual tone of the hunky-dory piece
To prevent the undone, collapsing roof,
Shielding the oppressive heat, scorched with no toupee.
Could not let out a single word, even for a moment. For
Disdained by upholsterers, for the paraplegics deserved

   no couch.
Like perturbing death that took toll on all strong men,
They dashed and hid silently in the ageless, deserted scrublands.
Now, wait for the gross adversity.
Soon, the looming strength will putrefy the uncovered pulp.
And you! This will be the most favored coin.
Blanc-mange and massage; retain the brittleness.
Founder invented the brocades that flashed the subway.
Rejected coin that brought the famous sounds.
They waved heartily in their glass houses.
He would say all to make all gloomy.
At random to the ill fated who suffered from amnesia.
This, the counter of Nobel Prize,
It ran for no noblemen.
Later for the wicked, the ruined boy.

Some out their casement windows
Kissed hard and kissed hard,
Cast down the strangled, chubby cheeks.
Watched carefully at the devaluated coin
Not e'en ranked to a farthing.
Realization, be of a wealthy nation.

Veil

Lift up the veil,
Host of some homeless soldiers.
Actual protocol of worship?
This, the malevolent honor,
I thought was to adore, respect.
He gave us this day
Every day.
Behind the twisted, kinky hair,
Can you lift up this veil?
Even if it's restoration of the symbol,
The greatest tower.
You already ran fast, deserted
The greatest tower.
Man oeuvre candidly might fall,
A victim before deserted.
Unroll your tongue.
Can't be led on ingenuity.
Of course we've got you.
We know the hoax.
Husky, hiatus blended
Might cause blockage.
Why hurt the voice box?
I know,
Could be building the rugged piece of bread.
Sorry, the unusual show of impiety.
You've built on the molten East Coast rock
Where the entire toothless regime turned their backs
To resist.

Before even you compromise the formula,
Doc shivered and fell on the ground.
We'll try and sing only
When you'll lift up the veil.
Not even will it appease the dead.
Is when will dress the veil.
From the vestments' closet,
Safe till the end of this time.

Beyond the Shadow

Beyond that same shadow,
Most hidden, that same feel.
Each day before the sun went down.
Flowed in that same soul
As plain waters down the fall.
Started as they stood by the gate,
Held possibilities at stake.
Ceased, that long political history
Of ages, ages, and ages.
Never knew all came and went.
Remained the possibilities again, and what we had?
Much admired by this silence.
Never provoked this moment; the feeling inside.
Enough proven by storms that strike the sea,
Beyond the shadow of iota.
Though irascible, to only who felt it mattered.
They were grounded by the torrential flow,
Rained, stained, and wet their feeble heart muscles.
My masterpiece to free and multiply.
Not insinuate, those who shared.
Greatness coveted by those sunbathed near the continental beach.
Beyond the shadow it came down.
Cover, hide the uncommon bareness.
This receding spot away. From
The palpable, poisonous shadow hunters.
The discriminative, this torturous singe.
Tough, may go through and through. Also
Beyond this same shadow.

I Pray

You settled right on top of the christening and the mingling clouds.
Open this tough fist that busted out in cherry flame.
I would only like to see
The treasure you compressed under the chilled magma.
Ride with me to that very disabled place,
Far, far away to fly with Grandpa, beyond the yellowing sun,
And a distance from the typhoon-infested gorge.
From this belittled deities whose tongues slipped misfortunes.
From the fortunate waves of the smiley Caribbean.
Walk with me and teach me, pray.
I pray.

"Oh very pleasant," if not the eye-catching maid on my wedding day.
The bitter sight is soared to the extreme limit at the end's edge.
Can you just give me out on bond?
I will disburse out through the most rumored prayer of redemption,
To only ask for succor so close to the late king's palace.
I will dress in a gown well-guarded and surrounded adversely by
    pom-pom,
Just to let you know how trembled I am beneath the mischief under
    the sky.
"To reward and also restrain you from complete unrelated mishaps."
"Large, advantageous strides only seek in the nick time."
Walk with me and teach me, pray.
I pray.

Give me undoubtedly fast-blowing and rolling wheel of reason,
The strapping ardor to brawl and brawl back and not to cave in spinelessly.
The virtuoso, that pliable mind, not the will to get boggy in animosity.
The out-of-sight riches, not the contentment of the rotten flesh.
Vision in point, not the flashlights that will scare away the unbecoming
    mole.
The heightened, admirable inspiration of touch and cause trouble to the
    untouchables.
Walk with me on the well-laid comfort of the woven, woolen red carpet.
Cast out the nothingness and accredit the vacuum with upbeat traits.
Please call me out. I never want to be completely discarded.
Walk with me and teach me, pray.
I pray.

Cast Dice

In soutanes and surplices.
Cast away claims based on stoicism.
Was demise and a piercing silver blade.
All was before the mentioned dark day came.
Them who juddered their muffled, hysterical juniors.
Misanthropists gave up, wanted to leave almost immediately.
With the potency of the hanging poppers, they conceded!
The ideology was stoic irony.
Ran back with inclined, loaded heads.
Narrated all with sagacity.
Lullabies made the brat higher and higher.
Abandoned all for forgiveness, in the name …
Cast about this and in our times.
Time for rowdy beggars to gulp down.

Dice that was cast by great men of the day,
Minds who thrilled of queen's English
In front of cast illustrious procession.
This stygian system is in immense snags.
The tight fisted and deeds inimical to prosperity?
Set not to go. For
Who will guard the goods and the chattels?
The woes and the cartels?
Cogitate on the laid founders
And those who are still here.
Howbeit, the loyalists and PAs.
Rapporteurs who lampooned dignitaries rhetorically.
Groundless, we'll never need you.

For one in the queen's counsel.
Cast them off after the fierce inferno. Eventually
They secretly headed down the perplexing avenues.
            "Now the die has been cast."
Spirit of loyalty to touch Africa.
Not skive, sprinkle from stoup.
Laudatory discourse! Not at all
Kept rolling, rolling, rolling,
Anaesthetized and covered the brain,
Sensitized acute pain.
Now, time for multilingual practitioner,
Inauguration of the first millennium party.
Philatelists munching in their pizza huts.
Dirigible dogs outside the lordly des res
Looked up the angelic sky.
Entreaty, not closure of the pizzeria.
Might have found a solace.

Do we really know about death?
Or in deep confusion after matricide?
Dice with death.
Numbness, emergence from the massive.
Pertinacity, thoughts of their own.
Burning vow slapped their blotched faces.
The discriminating call of the potters.
Maniacs of the classic feedback.
Just a glance at the peculiar treasure.
Rejection of the real one. And so
Need shade no tears. If only I could
Smear the collar of the foolish scholar.
Dawned on Kit-Mikayi.
Only for the heroes at the corner of the greatest fortunes.

The touch to the poor soul. Facilitate
New urn for the licking porridge.
Illicit bred with no prudence.
Orphan's song before the rituals.
Toss the coin in that far afternoon
Final rolls cast, the dice.